The Story I Told My Mother

The Story I Told My Mother

Jennifer Gravley

Poems & an Essay

TWELVE WINTERS
a literary project

Published by Twelve Winters, a literary project.

P. O. Box 414 • Sherman, Illinois 62684-0414 • twelvewinters.com

The Story I Told My Mother was first published by Twelve Winters in 2023. It is also available in other editions.

Cover and interior page design by TWP Design.

Cover art copyright © 2016 Erin Lyndal Martin. *Blue Angel*, alcohol ink on yupo. Used by permission. All rights reserved.

ISBN
978-8-9891086-0-2
Printed in the United States of America

for Moma,
who took me to the library

Acknowledgments

Grateful acknowledgment is made to the editors of the following publications where some of these pieces first appeared.

Blast Furnace: "In This as in All Narratives"
Blue Mountain Review: "A mother won't go when her children are present.," "Some Rhyme, Some Afterlife"
burntdistrict: "Accident Involving Extrication"
Clementine (Unbound): "How to Talk to Your Mother," "My mother is a spider."
concis: "From"
North American Review: "Proposing a World without a Mother: Grief and Creative Nonfiction as a Sense-Making Tool"
Shot Glass Review: "I Think of You"
Southern Poetry Review: "Lament"
Rat's Ass Review: "Old People," "Possessions"

Contents

The Story I Told My Mother

Poems

In This as in All Narratives

You wait for your mother to yellow. She will become a photograph, and you will bear this. Plot your grief on graph paper. Graph your grief as plot. You ought to study narrative theory and thoroughly consider which self will undertake this performance. You maintain as you wait, as she maintains, persists. She anticipates holidays. Increased traffic, increased drinking, increased collisions and injuries and fatalities. There is wild hope in death. You know what to expect, in this as in all narratives. Events and people will worsen before they better. This speculative convalescence cannot be trusted. There is always someone doing more poorly. There is always someone closer to the hospital. You chart what you will regret not knowing, though there is time to know and impracticable words in your throat. You cannot tolerate proximity or the terrible breath that overtakes voice. Wait for your mother to become not your mother, for the changes in skin and skull that will undo her. Wait for your mother to yellow. She will become a photograph, and you will bear this.

How to Talk to Your Mother

Ignore her. Say something smart. Shut your mouth. Turn your face to the wall. Be always in a different room when you cry. Ignore her questions. Clip your sentences bare. Allow her a goodbye when you leave. Wave from the car as she stands on the porch and then look ahead into traffic, opening your mouth to mumble-shout lyrics you can't understand. Call your mother so she knows you're alive. Call your mother and say uh-huh so she knows you're there. Lie down on the bed with the phone. Fall asleep. Call your mother. Say uh-huh, uh-huh. Lie down on the bed and cry, a different room after. Ignore the impulse to call your mother. Prepare to talk to your mother. Clip out bits of your life. Call your mother. Uh-huh. Fall asleep and pretend you didn't. Allow her a hello when you arrive. Tolerate her questions. Say something smart and regret it. Turn your face. Turn on the radio in the car. Wave. Call your mother so she knows you're alive and in bed. Ignore the words you can't clip bare. These words turn their faces to the wall. Call. Call your mother when dinner is about ready. Call your mother from work and say, I'm at work. Call your mother from your bed, poised to sleep or to cry. Ignore her as she talks. Ignore the impulse to question your mother. Call her. Waver. Ignore her as long as you can. Uh-huh. Call your mother so you know she's alive.

My mother is a spider.

My mother is a spider, silent and waiting. My mother is a spider inside a coat sleeve in the closet. She crouches in shadow in the toe of my shoe. She lives in the dark without worrying about her eyes. My mother can feel the smallest breeze, find any crack near a ceiling or floorboard. She adores corners. She has never asked anyone to bring her food or water. My mother inhabits the space between a file and the paper in it. She gains entrance to every box I have ever saved to move farther away from her. She mills about stairwells and entrances. My mother is a spider tattooed on the arm of a man who plays drums in his basement. The hair on her legs is his hair. My mother is a spider hanging from a tree. My mother is a spider in my bed. My mother is a spider tucked inside the mouth of a pillowcase. She lives in woodpiles and in outbuildings. All the things my grandmother said are tucked inside her mouth. My mother is a spider with a sac. Her sac contains me. My mother has a particular idea of housekeeping. She appears still, symmetrical. To stand next to her is to show your mathematical work. My mother is a spider inside my mind.

Old People

Old people want to kiss you, and they do. This is how you learn your lips will one day turn to paper. When you are older and can pick out and pay for lace underwear, a woman will wrap the underwear in paper like the lips of old people, just barely pink, thin enough to see shadows, shapes through, given to wrinkle. You will learn, through community educational programming, that painters sometimes apply this paper to canvas and paint over it. You will learn that something without texture can create it elsewhere—but not until it is too late for you. Old people want their things wrapped in paper. You open the dresser drawers of every old person you know. You go through the cabinets they display their old dishes in in dust. Every old person has the hair of their mother in a tiny envelope. Old people want you to eat expired candy, and you do. Old people want you to remember something about them. They shape the stories they want with their lips. Your hands tear at candy papers as you chew. You chew in your dreams at night, each tooth grinding away at some other. Your teeth grind at something every old person knows—it is too late for you.

From

I am from bruised thigh, junk drawer, box of borax on the top shelf. I am from vowel hard to pronounce, disordered creek bottom, bloody heel. I am from set of three. I am from formula, jar of baby teeth, sharp-bearded fish. I am from February, from Saturday, from many specifications of the abstractions time and space. I am from hand of my mother, bone of my mother's ear, mother of my mother's mother. From a tome of like characters. From filth, from undesirable car parts, from trundled spoilage.

Accident Involving Extrication

Head south in winter, watch for Dalton
and the back roads home.
Head for the house where the trees grew
switches more than leaves,
head for where your head must switch
off your heart to get through the day,
head through the darkening day to
the encroaching night of hard-knotted
sleep in the house with the off furnace.
Head into ragged breath and clutched
abdomens and swollen feet and unbendable
knees. Head where no one can lift over five
pounds or the deadening spirit you drag
behind you like a shadow,
head to where you knew you'd never
have children, to where all you can
hear is your sister crying.
Head to the median where you can already
see the metal bent, hear the radio report:
an accident involving extrication.

Possessions

You have wanted to lose many things and failed: your sister, then the children and dogs of neighbors. The fever that your eyes swam in like lava for days as you combined sentences on blackboards and crawled back to your apartment to die. You have seen your father undone by hoarding, every unkindness festering into a tight foul knot in the rag rug he carries inside him. This rug is where you learned to press your sitz bones into the ground. You have packed house—boarded planes—every time you felt anxiety knocking. Years after each winnowing, the boxes returned, in the mail or down the ladder from your parents' attic. Your mother tapes names on the smallest of possessions, but you and your sister do not turn them over when she leaves the room. You do not want to know what death will grant you. In the end, you will be lucky to get out with your teeth.

Other People's Narratives

All summer long it was the summer your mother would die.
You opened your mouth and laughed, read novels,
talked to other people's mothers. All summer long
you fretted about the job you were told you'd lose
all summer long. You saw films in air-conditioned theaters,
let other people's narratives summon anxiety and tears.
You took more photos of a rabbit thirsty for snow-cone drippings
than you did of your mother on her birthday
because it seemed like it would be summer all summer long.

A mother won't go when her children are present.

A daughter said, *Momma, I'm leaving.*
She shut the door from the inside,
crawled back through the house
and lay underneath the bed that held
her through childhood. Her belly breathed
against the floor against her will.
She thought, *Let this one be the last,*
thought, *Let this one be the last,*
all morning in the other room.
When the nurse called, *She's gone,*
she lay for a while, turned her head
on her neck. The carpet under the bed
felt like nothing anyone would want
their feet on. The bed skirt had no color
and hung like a succession of hands.
She was tucked in some envelope.
Every space she occupied would now be
darker, thicker at the seam. When she could
see the dresser again, her face somewhere
over her body, this would be real. This would
be the world without a mother. Mirrors
would hang on walls and show her what
was already the past as soon as she looked into them.

Am I dying right now?

Am I dying right now? Yes. No,
not the way you will be.
Wait with us a few hours.
Friends want to come see you
in the bed you will die in
while you still wake up
when we call your name.
Let us put our hands
on your arm and see your eyes
open. Let us practice
in the daylight closing
our eyes against your face.
Your mouth will close
when they stitch it
from inside, the thread
from a spool so much like
ones you pulled from.
What casket can bear
the weight of your body
so small now, your hands
empty of pens and needles.
What invisible thread can stitch
us to the bodies we leave
behind like each other.
You will come to me
all the nights of my life,
asking this one question,
yes and no, for you are
always now dying and

always blooming inside
me, fighting against death
with your hand to paper,
writing, writing to me.

Some Rhyme, Some Afterlife

Mourning lights the room like church.
Is this song that fills our throats?
Can we stutter through common meter
into some rhyme, some afterlife?
Mourning lights the room like balloons
drifting ceiling to floor, a little less,
a little less. Our faces take expression
from our hands, the clasp, the shudder.
Mourning lights the room like spoons
heaping salt into the bowls of our hearts.
Mourning lights the room like Mother
pulling the covers, pulling us with her.

I think of you.

One loss swallows another, growing its jaws
to embody death and death and death.
Loss limbers, loosens its wispy arms, legs.
Loss is a mass noun, uncountable even
when I count you and you. Loss is a skin
over skin, over eyes, over the pads of fingers
and toes which never warm. It is the worst
kind of blanket. It cannot untangle, unknot.
There are no corners. It is sewn by hand.

Lament

Seek no comfort in other people's children—
their easy intimacies, the names they call
their mothers when sick, when in distress, in discord.
Seek no comfort in food. Sugar sharp on the tongue,
that shock through the blood, that there is blood,
that it's you—a mistake. Seek no comfort in rest.
Sleep is a bloodletting, the dead always at you.
Seek no comfort in the daylight. The sun is a wound.
Nor in your body. Was your mother not young once?
Did she not bare her legs in short skirts?
Seek no comfort in the sky. Seek no comfort
in the earth. All the world and everything in it—
already marked for death, marked before you,
before you sought comfort in it, and marked after you.

Construction

Made of grief, of the dirt
under nails. Made mostly
of emptiness, the space
between the parts of everything.

Are the stars real anymore?

Is there a sky beyond the one
we saw together?
The sky that isn't a sky here
never darkens to pinholes.
Tonight it spiderwebs
behind clouds, the moon
a marble grave marker,
hard fat belly of death.

No Spring

Branches, swallow your buds. I want no
spring, no blooms but bruises.
Turn back black, trees. Bare scrawn
against gray sky. Grass, grow down
into the mud. Burrow like a casket.

Back from the Dead

Summer advances by adding
a smidgen. One day my nephew spells his name
with a silent "r" at the end. When the dog stays
under the porch too long, we stomp and holler
to bring her back from the dead. The attic surrenders
its jars to the pantry. The jars surrender their hollow.
Accumulated housework tenders itself to window light.
For coming so late, the night deepens itself with howls,
clouds its stars. All the men in my family outlive their women.

Essay

Proposing a World without a Mother: Grief and Creative Non-fiction as a Sense-Making Tool

INTRODUCTION

Problem.

To put it simply, "parents die as we age" (Safer 49). I am an outlier in this century, as most people lose their mothers when they are between forty-five and sixty-four years old (Safer 49). I was thirty-seven. But to put it more simply, parents die. Mothers die. My mother died.

> *All summer long it was the summer your mother would die, but you didn't know it. You were distracted by the universi-ty's decision to close the scholarly press where you worked, the backlash. You went to your first writers' conference at Sewanee, right off the highway along the way home.*

But we expect that our parents will die, abstractly, at some point. The problem, therefore, is not death but life; the problem, the unresolved difficulty, is how to go on living after a loved one's death. And worse, the problem is an inherently personal and specific one.

> *It is absolutely wrong that anything should change. It is absolutely wrong that anything should stay the same. This includes you. This applies exclusively, at heart, to you.*

Question.

But even while we feel we cannot go on, we know that people do and that we likely will as well.

This is what you write the first time you write it, that first night: "This is the world without a mother." It was already difficult to remember her face before she was sick. You knew her voice would go, too, fraying at the edges until it would become more made up than remembered.

The world is full, as much as we might not want it to be, of anecdotal evidence. Perhaps we ask ourselves what tools others have used or created in order to go on. Selfishly, the question is: How do I go on with living, every day in its everydayness, after the death of my mother?

This is the world without your mother—too much the same—a world of breath, a world where people open and close their mouths, their eyes.

Thesis Statement.
Or, Doesn't Writing It Make It True?

You haven't written about your mother's death. You are afraid to write. Writing makes it true. Writing means you are alive, that you are going on somehow, so you don't do it.

People make sense of their grief through the same methods they use to make sense of their worlds and lives generally; they go on by engaging in those same meaningful activities that allow them to go on. As a writer, I expect that exploring my grief through creative nonfiction will allow me to figure something out about that grief, about my mother's death, that will in turn allow me to go on, if only for a while,

Your therapist says you will probably miss your mother more as time goes on. That for adult children who live some distance from their parents, it's normal not to see them for months at a time, so it doesn't hit you all at once.

if only until I must write something else that will allow me to go on for a while.

About a year after your mother's death, you develop a lot of anxiety. Not that anyone could accuse you of not being a worrier already, but you feel anxiety in your body all the time. You tell your husband at dinner that you might flunk out of library school. You lie awake in bed, your heart beating fast, thinking of alternate routes downtown so you can avoid the hill you've driven every day since you moved to Missouri. You go back to therapy. Your therapist points out that you've stopped all your anxiety-releasing activities. You tell her you will think about writing. You admit that running three times a week is something you could easily do, but when you try it is painful to start over, and you are not even sure you want to run. Perhaps running is a pre-"bad year" activity. You think of it, refer to it, as "the bad year." Now it is more than one year after the bad year, and you are thinking about what you can do to feel more like yourself, but you don't care enough to do those things yet. You start to get rid of the pre-bad-year clothes because they remind you of the bad year. You start to get rid of the first post-bad-year clothes because they remind you of the bad year.

Statement of Significance.
Or, As the Creative Writers Say, "What's at Stake?"

What is at stake for all of us in our individual grief is ourselves and our worlds. Why then a public account of private grief? The way we understand grief best—or second best to personal experience—is the way we understand everything second best, through the particular stories of others' experiences. As a person, "[my] task in [my] own mourning and grieving is to fully recognize [my] own loss, to see it as only [I] can" (Kübler-Ross and Kessler 31).

When the dreams come, your mother does not know she is dead. In the dream that is like a dream of dreams, she is in the car with you on the way to her own burial. You don't want to get there. You don't want her to find out the grave is hers. Your sister tells you that she dreams of her tongue splitting, falling out in pieces, and you have one sympathy dream like this for her,

It started with your tongue swelling. You knew it was from diet soda. You didn't want them to operate. You told them what had happened to your mother.

They said they had to do it anyway.

Your tongue swole up so much it was like a second tongue had formed on top—you peeled it off.

They said they still had to do it.

You didn't want them to cut up your arm and leg just to die. You asked if they would just cut your tongue out and be done with it.

They said they had to do it.

but you return to your own dreams, unable to share even this aspect of grief with another person.

As a writer, I know that my story is significant because all of our stories are; the challenge is to present that story so that readers experience a bit of it with me, to contribute to the written record of the common—and painfully unique—human experience.

You pack a large suitcase, plan on staying a while. You pack about ten dresses, knowing one of them will be the dress you wear to your mother's funeral, but you will not make that decision now. You pack several notebooks, and the one with baby blue, aquamarine, and lime flowers on a gray background becomes the one. The notebook of your mother's death.

Purpose.
Or, (Write It!)

This essay aims to illustrate one person's struggle with grief through the form of creative nonfiction. Generally, I hope that my writing will fulfill the promise of why I think we all read—to be made to feel.

When your brother-in-law picked you up at the airport, your mother was in the E.R. The day before, a doctor had performed a biopsy on her tongue to confirm that the new tumors were cancerous, and now they wouldn't stop bleeding. Your mother on the bed in the E.R. looked tiny, little child legs kicking under the hospital blanket. At 61, she had shrunk four inches from the height noted in her senior memory book. She had lost forty pounds from her pre-cancer weight. She was as tiny as you now. Your mother was unable to close her mouth, the tumors needing room. A thick bloody saliva poured from her mouth. There was a smell around her. The biopsy to confirm cancer required by insurance? She was dead in two days. No one ever received the official results.

And as Robert Frost famously said, "No tears in the writer, no tears in the reader. No surprise for the writer, no surprise for the reader" (777). It is difficult to write something meaningful without figuring something out, and what I hope to figure out is otherwise inarticulable, the knowing or feeling or slight internal movement that the writing itself creates.

Scope and Limitations.

This essay is a personal reflection and journey into my particular grief over my mother's death.

Your mother had a notebook, too. When the tumors' swell prevented her speech, she wrote in a red wide-ruled one-subject notebook. Few pages were left. Five pages have her handwriting on them. Nine are blank. Your sister wanted to throw it out, called it "morbid," but you couldn't let go of her last words. It's a weird blessing and curse, to have her last few thoughts in their exact form but at the expense of her being able to say them. At the end she writes in all caps because it is easier. She was just getting some strength back in her right hand where they cut muscle from the forearm to remake her tongue.

As the journey will be lifelong, this essay can only capture one attempt to reconcile my grief with the mundane yet inescapable imperative to go on.

Definitions.

Or, Words Are All We Have.

Mourning is how we present our grief on the outside, or how society expects us to present our grief, "the external part of loss" (Kübler-Ross and Kessler 115).

When the funeral home people came to collect your mother, they wheeled her from her bedroom into the living room on a stretcher. They paused by the piano, the front door open, and made you say goodbye, even though you had been in the house with her body for hours, waiting. They had wrapped her in a sheet but left her face uncovered, her eyes still open, her mouth open, full of cancer.

Though we may no longer, as a rule, wear black, we find ourselves with expectations to fulfill just the same. A Facebook status relaying the time of death or of visitation or of funeral services is as clear an act of mourning.

At the funeral home, you and your sister and your aunt wanted a closed casket, but after a while, Daddy decided she would've wanted it open, so it was opened, and you had to see your mother's face in death again. They had closed her eyes. When your great-aunt arrived from Alabama, she stood with you near the casket for a long time and reached in and petted your mother's hands.

Grief is the feeling of bereavement, the sadness, the emotion itself (Kübler-Ross and Kessler 115, Attig 33).

Seeing Halloween hand towels at Kohl's and thinking how much your mother would like the green one—Frankenstein's monster's face. Realizing that she is not alive to receive the package in the mail.

Grieving is the internal counterpart to mourning, the everyday labor of coping with loss (Kübler-Ross and Kessler 115, Attig 33).

Thinking at Christmas, "Just get through this." Drinking a bottle of wine and vomiting into the toilet.

One night you drink a bottle of wine, not quick quick but too quick, and you are sick, lying on the floor of the little half-bath on the other side of the wall from the television. After a bout, you stay over the bowl and sob. Your husband asks what's wrong, and you're indignant that you should have to say what is wrong when what is wrong is what will be wrong forever. It's not fair, you say instead. It's not fair.

Telling yourself there's no birthday card coming in the mail. Erasing your mother's name,

Definition.

You will call your mother your mother. This bit of linguistic distance makes the essay possible, it makes you possible in this moment. At some point in childhood, as part of the larger project of realizing that your accent marked you and trying to emulate the middleclassness of your teachers, you would refer to your mother as your "mom" to select classmates. All of your real friends called their own mothers "Momma," and it would be uppity to pretend you did otherwise. Now it's been so long that to call her "my momma" to anyone except those you grew up with seems as false as those first "my mom"s probably did. In your head and in your heart, she is always "Moma," the way she taught you to spell it. You tried once to use this spelling—the only true one—in a story in one of your early workshops, and you were rightly called out for it. The nonstandard spelling was confusing and distracting for readers. But every "your mother" on the page stands for a "Moma" in the internal world that this essay only scratches at in the dark.

Genita Gravley, from your passport.

Assumptions.

It is assumed that the loss of a parent is a sad event that produces intense grief and takes a significant amount of time, probably the rest of the bereaved individual's life, to process.

You assumed that you'd want to write about your mother's death, so you packed notebooks.

Your mother was not something to write about.

You brought your laptop.

Your mother was not a topic; she was not a theme.

Your mother was the only person in the world to call you "baby."

You brought pens.

Outline of Steps to the Argument.
Or, Begin to Tell the Story of Your Mother's Death.

Because I experience grief in fragments, in pieces, in jagged moments or images from memory, I write about my grief in fragments, allowing the content to fit inside this form

The morning of the day your mother would die, you and your sister awoke to the sound of her yelling at Daddy for doing the laundry wrong. This fussing seemed a good sign, something to get you up and out of the spare bed where you had slept.

as every piece of writing requires structure. The reader needs it to make sense of the argument, and the writer needs it to help formulate the argument, even if the argument is as personal and evolving as, this is the story that allows me to get through the day.

All day your mother insisted on figuring out the appointment she had the next day, when to leave, who was driving. There was no point in going, but the hospice nurse said to go along, to go through the battle of grinding and feeding her usual medications through the tube, but to stop feeding her the liquid nutrition. That you were only feeding the cancer.

In this form of an academic proposal, I explore the intersection of my own experiences and my own craft with current concepts in the fields of grief theory and creative writing.

REVIEW OF LITERATURE

Introduction.

The subject of my essay is grief and the method of exploration is creative nonfiction. I read the literature on both. I begin with the subject itself. Theories on grief may suggest valuable approaches to the craft of creative writing. By exploring how creative nonfiction and essays work, I develop my own methodology.

Literature on Grief and Grieving.

One cannot escape Kübler-Ross's theory of the stages of grief; the chain of denial, anger, bargaining, depression, acceptance is ubiquitous in pop culture. Although the theory of these stages is meant to provide the bereaved a way to think about and name their feelings, they are commonly misunderstood to represent a universal and set order of grieving (Kübler-Ross and Kessler 7).

Your mother's surgery and tongue reconstruction make you angry. It was no small thing—removing slice after slice of tongue until the sample came back clean, removing muscle from her right arm, her writing hand since her left arm muscle was too weak, to reconstruct it, removing a patch of skin from her thigh to cover the wound on her arm. It took the whole month she lived afterward to start to recover. She still had the feeding tube in her stomach when she died. She was just starting to be able to eat baby food. She had left the house one time not for a doctor's appointment. When the cancer came back, the new doctor said there was never any hope that it wouldn't, not with the kind of cancer and her anti-rejection medications; he didn't know why they had done the surgery at all.

Because the bereaved do not all undergo the same journey with five set phases, some argue that the concept may be "dangerous. Perhaps it may do more harm than good" (Bonanno 22). An alternate way of thinking about grieving patterns is in terms of "reactions," the most common of which Bonanno identifies as chronic grief, recovery, and resilience (6–8).

Despite increasing awareness that the stages model is not descriptive of a one-size-fits-all lockstep of grieving, the idea of stages or steps remains in the idea of grief work. The idea that "grief is necessarily lengthy and debilitating" remains widespread, along with the idea that "the only way out is to work through it—in a series of stages, steps, tasks, phases, passages, or needs" (Konigsberg 40). In fact, many of the tasks "grief work" theories demand sound reminiscent of Kübler-Ross's stages. Lindemann's tasks include giving up attachment, adapting to the loved one's absence, and forming new connections; Parkes and Weiss's tasks include understanding and accepting the loss, as well as forming a revised sense of self; Worden's tasks include accepting the loss, dealing with the tumult of emotions, adapting to the loved one's absence, and giving up attachment (Attig 47).

You try to change. You decide to go to library school. You go with impure motives. You go not because you want to go to library school but because you do not want to do other things. What you do want is time, and you hear that library school is unchallenging. You hear that librarians love their jobs. The program is two years, two years of being on hold. You have been to grad school before, and you know that it's a kind of suspended animation: that for X number of years, no one expects you to work an unsatisfying office job for 40 hours a week, that you can return to the kind of life where you nap, where you write down your dreams and turn them into short short stories. You hope that you will be changed but that you will be the same person.

You change without trying. You gain the dead-mother weight of ice cream and chocolate candy and bags of chips—an apple, like your mother.

For a while you try to think to yourself, your mother is under the ground, to be blunt about it, to not forget in some moment of living that she is not. You try to tell yourself this when you want to eat ice cream because you are sad. Your mother is under the ground. You mother will never eat anything ever again. But you eat the ice cream.

You are laid off from your job. Your days lose their structure; your weeks, their pattern. You already have the kind of life where you can nap and write short short stories, but you do not. You do not write.

Safer believes this work to be rewarding beyond the movement toward a new normalcy from debilitating grief. She states, "Every adult whose parents die is entitled to death benefits. They are your 'deathrights,' part of your legitimate inheritance" (Safer 205). Even more conventional thought is that relearning ourselves and our worlds is a way of putting ourselves back together, of going on (Attig 105, 116). At the same time, loss recalls loss; it is impossible to grieve only the present loss when past losses stir and those hard-won adaptive changes feel like loss as well (Kübler-Ross and Kessler 73).

You try to stay the same. Your mother took you and your sister to the library every Saturday. She let you read whatever you wanted. You started a book in the car on the way home or standing in line to check out if there was one. She let you read while eating a sandwich in the living room when you got home. When you were in high school, she would drive you to the next county closer to Atlanta to go to their bigger library. If you become a librarian and she never knows about it, it's not something that would be surprising. The potential was always there. Would she be happy that you

*would be setting off to spend so much time in places where
you were perhaps happiest together?*

*You stay the same person without trying. Everywhere
you go, there you are, alive, and your mother is under
the ground. You enter the unchallenging library pro-
gram and lie awake at night fretting that you will fail
every assignment.*

Literature on Creative Nonfiction.

In thinking about creative nonfiction, I will consider various
types of essays with equal interest toward what they offer us as
readers and writers. All essays worth writing—or reading—offer
their writers a chance at encountering a truer self, if not a truth.
Epstein states, "I have often felt, in fact, that the only coherent,
consecutive thought I am capable of comes about through my
own writing and through reading other writers" (21).

*After your mother's death, all of the things that you enjoyed
become unpalatable. You stop running. You don't go to
yoga. You don't write. The running, the yoga—they can't
compete with sitting alone with your thoughts, with let-
ting the dread spiral in your belly. The writing is terrifying.
Unthinkable that you could write when your mother was
under the ground. And if you did, what might you write?
Wouldn't it be wrong to write about her? Wrong to ever
again write about anything else? And did you want to find
out what you might find out if you let yourself write?*

The metaphor of the essay as an experiment is common.
D'Agata says, "If essays are experiments then they are journeys,
too. . . . Why bother conducting an experiment at all if you know
what results it will yield?" (231).

38

Your mother died while you were about to make sandwiches. Your aunt and uncle had sent you and your sister to the grocery store, and it was a relief to be out of the house for half an hour. It was a relief to move among people who didn't know that you were waiting for your mother to die. It was difficult to pick out food. You had a hundred-dollar bill. You thought you were buying food for supper that night, maybe, but you knew you were buying food you would eat after your mother died. What would you like to eat after your mother died? You brought home bread, the makings for sandwiches, at least one frozen pizza, and fifty dollars.

Lopate says, "The essay is not, for the most part, philosophy; nor it is yet science. How seriously ought we to take its claims of being experimental? It lacks the rigor of a laboratory experiment; it does not hold on to its hypotheses long enough to prove them. But it is what it is: a mode of inquiry, another way of getting at truth" (xlv).

You and your sister put the groceries away and returned to your mother, who in the half hour could no longer sit up in bed. When you went back to the kitchen to tell Daddy she was gone, he couldn't believe it. He thought she had months, even when the tumors in her mouth stopped her from talking. He was making sandwiches that required slicing. He had something—a tomato, an onion—in his hand with the knife over the trashcan. He kept making the sandwich and ate it. You remember him making two.

Champion of the lyric essay, D'Agata defines it as "its own hybrid version of the [nonfiction] form. It takes the subjectivity of the personal essay and objectivity of the public essay, and conflates them into a literary form that relies on both art and fact, on imagination and observation, rumination and argumentation, human faith and human perception" (436). In the end, he defines the lyric essay as "an argument that has no chance of proving anything" (436). If we accept that, then why read or write such monstrous texts?

In lyric essays, readers are asked to do the work of figuring out potential conclusions; as Miller and Paola note, "the writer, by surrendering to the fragmented form, declines a foregone conclusion" (106). They argue that writers of lyric essays "must surrender to the writing process itself to show us the essay's intent" (107).

Much later, after the hospice nurse declared the death, after the funeral home brought the body through the living room—they don't close the eyes, they only do that on television—after the visitors and your aunt and uncle left, you told your brother-in-law that you would eat after he and your sister left so that they would leave.

An essay is often not even about what it proclaims to be about. No matter what a writer is exploring, they are always at heart exploring themselves.

You did not eat. You did not eat the next morning. All morning long in the funeral parlor you entertained guests. Eventually you went to the kitchen in the back where there were remnants of the food the women of your family's church had brought. You cut one-quarter of a grocery-store chocolate cake, tall, impeccable thick icing. You ate, thinking, your mother is under the ground, even though she wasn't yet, she was in the next room. You ate mainly the icing.

Epstein sets out that the distinguishing characteristic of the personal essay is that "all claims to objectivity are dropped at the outset, all masks removed, and the essayist proceeds with shameless subjectivity" (18). Lopate defines the "plot" of the personal essay as the writer delving closer and closer to honesty (xxv).

Now you have told the story of the your mother's death. You have gotten through it one time in writing, in words on a screen, in words that you can print and hold in your hands or tear with your hands.

What now? Can the reader mark your progress on Freytag's Pyramid, or are you the frustrating narrator, unchanging and stuck?

There is more to tell. There are better ways to tell it. You are a long way from any of those. You are one day closer to integrating the self that wants to be the same with the self that wants to be different, but you still don't believe that it can happen. You are one telling of the story closer to a telling that will make it hurt less but also one telling of the story closer to a telling that will make it hurt more, and that is essential.

METHODOLOGY

Or, What Can You Make of the Grief That Resides in Your Mouth But Words, a Story.

Telling the story of one's loved one's death or of one's own grief is a way to try to make sense. Kübler-Ross and Kessler liken it to detective work, seeking out the pieces of the puzzle that will help one eventually put it together: "Telling the story helps to re-create and rebuild structure" (63).

For a while, you think to yourself, This is the world without your mother. You think, This is what it's like to go to work in a world without your mother. You think, This is what it's like to go to the movies in a world without your mother. You think, This is what it's like to go for a run in a world without your mother. Each time you think this thought it helps you frame or reframe or build the world in front of you without her. It's like if you don't think it, you are pretending that the world has not changed when it has, when no one should be allowed for a moment to forget that it has.

Writing is a time-honored tradition of grief work. Writings "are concrete ways to celebrate beloved memories or to resolve tormenting ones. Artists conjure their parents in their work to bring them back, to lay them to rest, or to say what could never have been said in person" (Safer 131–132).

Your mother will never call you again.

Every message began, "Hey, baby, it's Moma."

Your first phone upgrade, the sales associate activates the new phone without warning you that it will delete most of your voicemails. It saves random ones—appointment reminders, messages from numbers not programmed into your phone, and only two from your mother. Both are from after the surgery to remove the original tumor, so her voice has that slurred, choking quality of her last month alive.

You call and complain and practically beg them—is there some kind of daily backup file?—but there's nothing they can do. The associate on the phone tells you that you can imagine that they had many of these in-

quiries after 9/11. You can imagine that, but it feels like cheating to make your tragedy seem small and personal. Everyone's tragedies are small and personal. That's why everyone is begging for a secret stash of voicemails.

This essay is less a way to lay my mother to rest than to keep her alive within me as I try to figure out how to reconcile my desire to change utterly with my desire to remain absolutely the same.

The grief theorists and the writers agree on the value of, the hardwiring for, storytelling. Bonanno says we generally manage bereavement well because we are "wired" with the skills to do so (198). Cron says, "We think in story. It's hardwired in our brains. It's how we make strategic sense of the otherwise overwhelming world around us" (8). For the bereaved writer, Cron's hypothesis that stories "often begin the moment a pattern in the protagonist's life stops working." feels gut-wrenchingly accurate (187).

The first birthday after your mother's death is your nephew's. He turns nine a week later and wants the family party that he's always had: cake and decorations. You take him to Wal-Mart and buy him the $70 video game he wants because he seems to truly want nothing else, and what else can you give him? Your niece wants a phone, and when you lie together on the extra bed in what you must now call your father's house, and she whines and says everyone else has one, you believe her, and you want her to have a phone. Two months later when your upgrade comes through, your send her your old iPhone and put a line for her onto your bill.

You had always thought about getting your mother a laptop and internet service. You think of how much she might have enjoyed it. You think she would have en-

joyed it far more than she would have, probably, but any amount that she would have enjoyed it, you never got around to giving her.

If the content of the project is to tell the story of my mother's death, of my initial attempts to do or to avoid the hard work of grieving, then I must find an appropriate form. The current freedom of form—D'Agata's suggestion that every essay is experimental no longer seems revolutionary—leaves me with many options (95). The best option is always the one that arises organically.

At the church, you sat through the preaching. It felt like a revival, more talk of your mother being saved and going home than of her life on earth, of her as individual person. Then everyone, row by row, went to view the body. This included the family, you and your family. You walked as a group near the casket, just a few feet away from the first bench, and then walked back. You had seen your mother's face inside the casket too much already, made up, the varnish on her nails, her mouth sewn shut over what you knew was still inside. Then the church, row by row, came to the family. You shook hands and hugged. You should've known who these people were, but you stopped going to church as a teenager and moved away and didn't come back. Then you sat in a row by the casket at the gravesite. Then you moved away while the work was done and came back when your mother was finally and fully under the ground.

When your sister orders flowers for her second birthday under the ground, she tells you the florist asked, "Is it a country grave?"

In my studies of the literature of grief theory and creative writ-

44

ing, I hoped that a common thread would emerge, and as discussed above, the idea of storytelling as a sense-making tool became that common thread. Because this comparison took place within the form of a proposal for an academic essay, I now utilize this received form as a way to integrate the research with my personal narrative. The narrative is interspersed, interrupts, exemplifies, and perhaps contradicts the proposal. The form of the proposal is doubly fitting because the work of storytelling in grief is to "propose" a new world, a new self.

I begin the proposal and its review of literature separately from the narrative essay.

You start this essay more than once. You start this essay without the notebook of your mother's death every time. For a while, you carried it with you, in case you needed to record some thought or memory. Then you put it away. Then you got it back out and put it next to the bed because of the dreams. It has stayed there, other notebooks and library books often on top of it. When you were growing up, the family bible—a big St. James with the words of Jesus in red—lay on top of the television (it lays there now), and you weren't allowed to put anything on top of it.

When both have reached a critical mass of words on the page, I print them out. Beginning with the proposal, I use scissors to cut the separate sections and make piles of them. I also cut each idea and quotation from the literature review draft and sort them into groups by discipline, then idea. After pasting these back together, I have a draft of the academic proposal.

You were in the room for your mother's last breath. Your sister knew it was coming, said she was gray about the mouth. You were there for her last breath but didn't realize it was her last at the time—you can only ever realize after, in the absence of another. Your sister was frantic on the phone with the hospice nurse. You were desperately trying to open the little bottle of morphine, which you were dripping into her feeding tube not for pain, because she complained of none the whole day, but to help relax the panic of not being able to breathe. Afterward, her face looked plastic, waxen, changed colors. Her eyes stayed a tiny bit open.

Then I go through the same process with my narrative fragments—printing, cutting, and sorting. Here there are multiple levels of sorting to be applied. What can be gained from a chronological approach? Do patterns of diction, of syntax, of theme, etc., emerge? Is it possible to sort the narrative fragments by direct correspondence to parts of the proposal itself, to form a sort of call and response?

Your mother wrote in her notebook "Am I dying right now?" Always the coward, you waited for your sister to say that it was between her and God. Did she feel God calling her home? She said no. Your sister later said she was lying. Not believing in God or home, you believe them both.

It became harder and harder to be in the room with your mother. "Don't cry and upset me," she wrote to your best friend from childhood. "It makes [it] hard to breathe."

Your mother wrote, "Can I open [my] mouth?" She hadn't been able to close her mouth in days.

Imagine your mouth closing itself with tumors.

In terms of the content of the narrative itself, I strive for honesty and try not to shy away from revealing what Bonanno calls "coping ugly" behavior, an evocative term for exactly what it sounds like (78).

> *After your mother dies, you spend two weeks at home with your father. One day while your niece and nephew are at school, you and your sister take your father loafering. You go into a gold mine, the kind of thing that you would have loved as children but never got to do. There was a gold rush in Georgia, the mountains washed away. You don hard hats and go into the mine, following a guide. You pay the extra money at the end to pan for gold, and you each go home with a little plastic tube of the gold flakes from your particular pans. It's harder work than one would think. Your haul ranges from two to three flakes. When you are still in the mouth of the mine, you take a photograph with your phone of your father and sister. They smile, and if you didn't know, looking at the photo, you would think they are happy.*

I try to keep telling the story when the story is recounting what stories best recount: "the battle between fear and desire" (Cron 126). Part of writing is wallowing—allowing oneself the luxury of thought and revision of thought as well as of the words themselves. Attig describes the attraction that "dwelling in the emotion grief" holds for some of us (36–37). This project flirts with that bittersweet dwelling, but the effort to create something out of it makes it an active dwelling.

> *The notebook of your mother's death is the anti-bible. You want to know it is there but buried. You want access to it without carrying it, without seeing it, without the conscious reminder of everything it contains in its record. You want to imagine that it is more complete than it is, than it can possibly be. You want to imagine that it contains your mother's death, that it will fix all the memories that have already*

faded, that it will give up more information each time it is read, that it will serve as a kind of bible for the child who could never believe but who would read and read and read.

Lopate cautions that "It is difficult to write analytically from the middle of confusion," but there is no other way to write from grief (xxxvii). Writing is always an activity at a remove, but "essayists write for the sake of preservation; in order to find solutions to problems, in order to remain intellectually, emotionally, or spiritually awake amidst the full rumbling fury of the world" (D'Agata 407).

On your first birthday after your mother's death, you force your husband to bake you a cake. Even though it's been many years since your mother baked you a birthday cake, you refuse to admit it's a world in which no one bakes you a birthday cake. Your husband bakes cookies, not cakes, but you buy cake pans in with the weekly groceries, and he gives it a good try. You eat the leftover icing from the container with a spoon. With your mother, there was no leftover icing and sometimes more than one container was required.

Writing is in fact a form of preservation of self.

The notebook of your mother's death is the notebook you do not let yourself write in anymore. It is the notebook with dotted lines instead of regular lines. It is the notebook with the funeral home's "in loving memory" card inside. It is the notebook you practiced writing "mother" in because it furthered the distance that writing already puts between writer and event. It is the notebook that you hoped could save you from grief.

You write this essay instead: the only way to live with or through anything—construct a story about it. And like all writing—revise. Find comfort in form, structure, pattern, indulge in breaking it.

Remembering overrides memories, so—

Tell yourself the story until you are in it.

NOTE

The form for a proposal was taken from:

Gibson, Twyla, and Mark Lipton. *Research, Write, Create: Connecting Scholarship and Digital Media*. Oxford UP, 2014.

WORKS CITED

Attig, Thomas. *How We Grieve: Relearning the World*. Oxford UP, 1996.

Bonanno, George A. *The Other Side of Sadness: What the New Science of Bereavement Tells Us About Life After Loss*. Basic, 2009.

Cron, Lisa. *Wired for Story: The Writer's Guide to Using Brain Science to Hook Readers from the Very First Sentence*. Ten Speed, 2012.

D'Agata, John, ed. *The Next American Essay*. Graywolf, 2003.

Epstein, Joseph. "The Personal Essay: A Form of Discovery." Introduction. *The Norton Book of Personal Essays*. Ed. Epstein. Norton, 1997, pp. 11-24.

Frost, Robert. "The Figure a Poem Makes." *Collected Poems, Prose, and Plays*. Library of America, 1995, pp. 776–778.

Konigsberg, Ruth Davis. *The Truth about Grief: The Myth of Its Five Stages and the New Science of Loss*. Simon & Schuster, 2011.

Kübler-Ross, Elisabeth, and David Kessler. *On Grief and Grieving: Finding the Meaning of Grief Through the Five Stages of Loss*. Scribner, 2005.

Lopate, Phillip. Introduction. *The Art of the Personal Essay: An Anthology from the Classical Era to the Present*, edited by Lopate. Anchor-Random, 1995, pp. xxiii–liv.

Miller, Brenda, and Suzanne Paola. *Tell It Slant: Writing and Shaping Creative Nonfiction*. McGraw-Hill, 2005.

Safer, Jeanne. *Death Benefits: How Losing a Parent Can Change an Adult's Life—For the Better*. Basic, 2008.

ABOUT THE AUTHOR

Jennifer Gravley has published widely, including in venues such as *Southern Poetry Review* and *North American Review*. She has an MFA from the University of Alabama, where she was a winner in the AWP Intro Journals Project in fiction and held a Teaching-Writing Fellowship. She has attended the Sewanee Writers' Conference and been awarded a residency from the Ragdale Foundation. Gravley, assistant director of an academic library, hails from the North Georgia mountains and now resides in the middle of the middle of the country with her husband and his plant.